A Paines Plough and Theatr Clwyd production

T0247471

HOW TO SPOT AN ALIEN

by Georgia Christou

The first performance of *How To Spot An Alien* took place on 2 June 2018 in Paines Plough's Roundabout at Theatr Clwyd.

Supported using public funding by
ARTS COUNCIL
ENGLAND

How To Spot An Alien

by Georgia Christou

Cast

JELLY	Charlotte O'Leary
JONJO	Jack Wilkinson
MUM/POLICEMAN/AUNT LEINA/ TAXI DRIVER	Katherine Pearce

Production Team

Direction	Stef O'Driscoll
Lighting	Peter Small
Sound & Composition	Dominic Kennedy
Co-Movement Director	Jennifer Jackson
Co-Movement Director	Simon Carroll-Jones
Assistant Director	Balisha Karra
Lighting Programmer	Tom Davis
Line Producer	Sofia Stephanou
Company Stage Manager	Caitlin O'Reilly
Technical Stage Manager	Wesley Hughes
Technical Stage Manager (Edinburgh)	Ben Pavey

GEORGIA CHRISTOU (Writer)

Georgia is a previous member of the Royal Court Young Writers' Group. Her first full-length play *Yous Two*, which was originally shortlisted for the Verity Bargate Award in 2015, ran at the Hampstead Theatre Downstairs earlier this year. She has also been selected as part of Channel 4's 4Stories scheme and is writing an original single drama which will shoot this year.

CHARLOTTE O'LEARY (Jelly)

Charlotte trained at The Royal Welsh College of Music and Drama.

Theatre credits include: *Under Milk Wood* (Watermill); *Hush* (Paines Plough); *Three Days in the Country, Dying for It, The Two Gentleman of Verona, Three Sisters* (Richard Burton Theatre Company).

Radio: *Torchwood* (Big Finish Productions).

JACK WILKINSON (Jonjo)

Jack trained at Drama Centre London.

Theatre includes: *Twelfth Night* (Shakespeare's Globe); *King Lear* (Northern Broadsides/UK tour); *Close the Coalhouse Door* (Northern Stage/UK tour); *Dreamplay* (The Vaults/HighTide); *David Copperfield* (Oldham Coliseum; nominated for Best Actor at MTA Awards); *All Of Me* (The Vaults); *Grimms Ditch* (The Print Works); *Larisa and the Merchants* (Arcola); *Deadkidsongs* (Theatre Royal Bath), and *The Good Soul of Szechuan* (Watford Palace Theatre).

TV: *Holby City, Doctors* (BBC) and *Marvellous* (Tiger Aspect).

Film: *The Love Punch* (Radar Films).

Radio: *Close the Coalhouse Door* (BBC).

KATHERINE PEARCE (Mum/Policeman/ Aunt Leina/Taxi Driver)

Katherine trained at The Royal Welsh College of Music and Drama.

Katherine's theatre credits include: *The Last Ballad of Lillian Billocca* (Hull Truck); *Low Level Panic* (Orange Tree; nominated for Best Actress Offie Awards 2018); *Husbands and Sons, Port* (National Theatre); *Husbands and Sons, Our Pals* (Manchester Royal Exchange); *Stab in the Dark, Chamber Piece, Streetcar Named Desire, Woyzeck, A Series of Increasingly Impossible Acts, Glitterland* (Secret Theatre Company at Lyric Hammersmith).

Television credits include: *Girlfriends, Vera* (ITV); *Three Girls, Young Hyacinth, Our Girl* (BBC).

Film credits include: *My Cousin Rachel* (Fox Searchlight); *England is Mine* (HonlodgeProductions); *The Last Photograph* (The Works International).

STEF O'DRISCOLL (Direction)

Stef is the Artistic Director of nabokov and previously the Associate Director at Paines Plough and at the Lyric Hammersmith.

For Paines Plough: *With a Little Bit of Luck* by Sabrina Mahfouz, *Hopelessly Devoted* by Kate Tempest, *Blister* by Laura Lomas, and as Assistant Director: *Wasted* by Kate Tempest.

For nabokov: *Last Night* by Benin City (Roundhouse/Latitude); *Box Clever* by Monsay Whitney (Marlowe Theatre/ Roundabout); *Storytelling Army* (Brighton Festival), and *Slug* by Sabrina Mahfouz (Latitude).

For the Lyric, as Co-Director: *A Midsummer Night's Dream*, as Associate Director: *Mogadishu* (Manchester Royal Exchange), as Assistant Director: *Blasted* – winner Olivier Award for Outstanding Achievement in an Affiliate Theatre 2011.

Other Director credits: *Yard Gal* by Rebecca Prichard – winner Fringe Report Award for Best Fringe Production 2009 (Ovalhouse); *A Tale from the Bedsit* by Paul Cree (Roundhouse/Bestival); *Finding Home* by Cecilia Knapp (Roundhouse); *A Guide To Second Date Sex* and *When Women Wee* (Underbelly/Soho) and as Assistant Director: *Henry IV* (Donmar Warehouse/ St Anne's Warehouse).

PETER SMALL (Lighting)

Peter studied Lighting Design at RADA. Peter's recent productions include *Plastic* (Poleroid Theatre, Old Red Lion) *All Or Nothing* (West End/UK tour); *Old Fools* (Southwark Playhouse); *Out Of Love*, *Black Mountain* (Offie nominated) and *How To Be a Kid* (Paines Plough/Orange Tree); *A Girl in School Uniform (walks into a bar)* (New Diorama; Offie nominated); *Fox* (Old Red Lion); *Memory of Leaves* (UK tour); *East End Boys and West End Girls* (Arcola/UK tour); *Electric*, *Politrix* (Big House Theatre); *Tom & Jerry* (EventBox Theatre, Egypt); *Cinderella* (Loughborough) and *The Venus Factor* (Bridewell).

DOMINIC KENNEDY (Sound & Composition)

Dominic Kennedy is a Sound Designer and Music Producer for performance and live events, he has a keen interest in developing new work and implementing sound and music at an early stage in a creative process. Dominic is a graduate from Royal Central School of Speech and Drama where he developed specialist skills in collaborative and devised theatre making, music composition and installation practices. His work often fuses found sound, field recordings, music composition and synthesis.

Recent design credits include: *The Assassination of Katie Hopkins* (Theatre Clywd); *Roundabout season 2017*, *With a Little Bit of Luck* (Paines Plough); *Ramona Tells Jim* (Bush); *And the Rest of Me Floats* (Outbox); *I Am a Tree* (Jamie Wood); *Box Clever* (nabokov); *Skate Hard Turn Left* (Battersea Arts Centre); *Gap in the Light* (Engineer); *Broken Biscuits*, *Roundabout season 2016* (Paines Plough); *The Devil Speaks True* (Goat and Monkey); *Run* (Engineer), and *O No!* (Jamie Wood).

JENNIFER JACKSON (Co-Movement Director)

Jennifer trained at East 15 and is a movement director and actor. Movement direction includes: *Queens of the Coal Age* (Royal Exchange); *Brighton Rock* (Pilot Theatre); *Parliament Square* (Bush/Royal Exchange); *Our Town* (Royal Exchange); *The Mountaintop* (Young Vic); *Out Of Love*, *Black Mountain*, *How To Be A Kid* (Paines Plough/Orange Tree/Theatr Clwyd & Roundabout tour); *Kika's Birthday* (Orange Tree); *Death of a Salesman* (Royal & Derngate); *The Ugly One* (The Park 90); *Phone Home* (Shoreditch Town Hall); *Why The Whales Came* (Southbank Centre); *Stone Face* (Finborough); *Debris* (Southwark Playhouse/Openworks Theatre); *Macbeth* (Passion in Practise & Sam Wanamaker Playhouse); *Silent Planet* (Finborough); *Pericles* (Berwaldhallen); *The Future* (The Yard/Company Three), *Other-Please Specify*, *Atoms* (Company Three).

As a performer she has worked with National Theatre, Bath Theatre Royal, Royal & Derngate, Lyric Hammersmith, Shoreditch Town Hall, Derby Theatre, Birmingham Rep, Southwark Playhouse & The Sam Wanamaker Playhouse. She is currently touring Bryony Lavery's adaptation of *Brighton Rock*.

SIMON CARROLL-JONES (Co-Movement Director)

Simon trained at East 15 Acting School. He is a theatre maker, movement director and actor.

Movement direction includes: *The Act* (The Yard/Company 3); *Bear and Butterfly* (Dani Parr/Theatre Hullabaloo); *Spring Awakening / Marigolds* (Brockley Jack/Outfox); *The Cycle Play* (East 15); *+-Human Response* (Roundhouse); *Tricycle Takeover / Mapping Brent* (The Tricycle).

Simon has taught movement at Central School of Speech and Drama, East 15 Acting School, and Identity Acting School.

As an actor Simon has worked with the RSC, Soho Theatre, The Royal and Derngate, Bath Theatre Royal, Shoreditch Town Hall, Tangled Feet Theatre, Theatre Hullabaloo, Hull Truck, Lyric Hammersmith, Battersea Arts Centre, Ovalhouse. Simon is an associate artist of Angel Exit Theatre, Moving Dust, Tangled Feet and Upstart Theatre.

Simon's solo show, *Marco*, will be touring in 2019 with James Blakey and Upstart Theatre.

BALISHA KARRA (Assistant Director)
Balisha studied at University of Birmingham (BA Hons in Drama and Theatre Arts).

Trainee Assistant Director: *A Midsummer Night's Dream* directed by Joe Hill-Gibbons (Young Vic/supported by Boris Karloff Foundation).

Assistant Director: *Present Laughter* by Noël Coward (Chichester Festival Theatre); *Freeman* by Strictly Arts (Belgrade Theatre Company UK tour, supported by Regional Theatre Young Directors Scheme).

Director credits: Besharam Project R&D (Derby Theatre); *Tamasha Scratch Night* (Writers Group/Rich Mix) and Foundry director for shows including *Mr Muscle*, *West* and *Confetti* (Birmingham REP).

CAITLIN O'REILLY (Company Stage Manager)
Caitlin is a freelance events/productions professional and has been working as a stage manager for the past nine years. Credits include: *Suppliant Women* (Actors Touring Company, Hong Kong Arts Festival); *Romeo and Juliet* (Orange Tree); *Beauty and the Beast* (Chichester Festival Theatre); *Dry Room* (Eldarin Young, Taiwan World Stage Design Festival); *Running Wild* (Michael Morpurgo, national tour), *Goosebumps Alive* (Tom Salamon, Vaults, Waterloo); *I Know All The Secrets In My World* (Tiata Fahodzi, national tour); *The 39 Steps* (Patrick Barlow, Criterion), and *Ben Hur* (Patrick Barlow, Tricycle) among many more.

PAINES PLOUGH

Paines Plough is the UK's national theatre of new plays. We commission and produce the best playwrights and tour their plays far and wide. Whether you're in Swansea or Sheffield, Glasgow or Gloucester, a Paines Plough show is coming to a theatre near you soon.

'The lifeblood of the UK's theatre ecosystem' *Guardian*

Paines Plough was formed in 1974 over a pint of Paines Bitter in the Plough pub. Since then we've produced more than 130 new productions by world renowned playwrights like Stephen Jeffreys, Abi Morgan, Sarah Kane, Mark Ravenhill, Dennis Kelly, Mike Bartlett and Kate Tempest. We've toured those plays to hundreds of places from Brisbane to Bristol to Belfast.

'That noble company Paines Plough, de facto national theatre of new writing' *Daily Telegraph*

In the past three years we've produced 30 shows and performed them in over 200 places across four continents. We tour to more than 30,000 people a year from Cornwall to the Orkney Islands; in village halls and Off-Broadway, at music festivals and student unions, online and on radio, and in our own pop-up theatre Roundabout.

With Programme 2018 we continue to tour the length and breadth of the UK from clubs and pubs to lakeside escapes and housing estates. Roundabout hosts a jam-packed Edinburgh Festival Fringe programme and brings mini-festivals to each stop on its nationwide tour, and you can even catch us on screen with *Every Brilliant Thing* available on Sky Atlantic and HBO.

Our *Come To Where I'm From* smartphone app is available free on iOS and Android, featuring 160 short audio plays from Olivier Award winners to first time writers.

'I think some theatre just saved my life' @kate_clement on Twitter

PAINES PLOUGH ⦿ ROUNDABOUT

'A beautifully designed masterpiece in engineering… a significant breakthrough in theatre technology.' *The Stage*

Roundabout is Paines Plough's beautiful portable in-the-round theatre. It's a completely self-contained 168-seat auditorium that flat packs into a single lorry and pops up anywhere from theatres to school halls, sports centres, warehouses, car parks and fields.

We built Roundabout to enable us to tour to places that don't have theatres. For the next decade Roundabout will travel the length and breadth of the UK bringing the nation's best playwrights and a thrilling theatrical experience to audiences everywhere.

Over the last five years Roundabout has toured the four corners of the UK, hosting over 2,000 hours of entertainment for more than 100,000 people.

Roundabout was designed by Lucy Osborne and Emma Chapman at Studio Three Sixty in collaboration with Charcoalblue and Howard Eaton.

WINNER of Theatre Building of the Year at The Stage Awards 2014

'Roundabout venue wins most beautiful interior venue by far @edfringe.'
@ChaoticKirsty on Twitter

'Roundabout is a beautiful, magical space. Hidden tech make it Turkish-bath-tranquil but with circus-tent-cheek. Aces.'
@evenicol on Twitter

Roundabout was made possible thanks to the belief and generous support of the following Trusts and individuals and all who named a seat in Roundabout. We thank them all.

TRUSTS AND FOUNDATIONS
Andrew Lloyd Webber Foundation
Paul Hamlyn Foundation
Garfield Weston Foundation
J Paul Getty Jnr Charitable Trust
John Ellerman Foundation

CORPORATE
Universal Consolidated Group
Howard Eaton Lighting Ltd
Charcoalblue
Avolites Ltd
Factory Settings
Total Solutions

Pop your name on a seat and help us pop-up around the UK:
www.justgiving.com/fundraising/roundaboutauditorium

www.painesplough.com/roundabout
#roundaboutpp

Paines Plough

Joint Artistic Directors	James Grieve
	George Perrin
Senior Producer	Hanna Streeter
General Manager	Aysha Powell
Producer	Sofia Stephanou
Assistant Producer	Harriet Bolwell
Administrator	Charlotte Walton
Marketing and Audience	
Development Manager	Jack Heaton
Production Assistant	Phillippe Cato
Finance and Admin Assistant	Charlotte Young
Technical Director	Colin Everitt
Trainee Administrator	Emanpreet Bhatti
Trainee Director	Balisha Karra
Production Placement	Eleanor Fitz-Gerald
Marketing Placement	Caitlin Plimmer
Admin Placement	Lily Ingleton
Big Room Playwright Fellow	Charley Miles
Press Representative	The Corner Shop PR
Graphic Designer	Michael Windsor-Ungureanu
	Thread Design

Board of Directors

Caro Newling (Chair), Ankur Bahl, Kim Grant, Nia Janis, Dennis Kelly, Matthew Littleford, Anne McMeehan, Christopher Millard, Cindy Polemis, Carolyn Saunders and Andrea Stark.

Paines Plough Limited is a company limited by guarantee and a registered charity.
Registered Company no: 1165130
Registered Charity no: 267523

Paines Plough, 4th Floor, 43 Aldwych, London WC2B 4DN
+ 44 (0) 20 7240 4533
office@painesplough.com
www.painesplough.com

 Follow @PainesPlough on Twitter

 Like Paines Plough at facebook.com/PainesPloughHQ

 Follow @painesplough on Instagram

Donate to Paines Plough at justgiving.com/PainesPlough

Theatr
Clwyd

Theatr Clwyd is one of the foremost producing theatres in Wales – a beacon of excellence looking across the Clwydian Hills yet only forty minutes from Liverpool.

Since 1976 it has been a theatrical powerhouse and much-loved home for the community. Now, led by the Executive team of Tamara Harvey and Liam Evans-Ford, it is going from strength to strength producing world-class theatre, from new plays to classic revivals.

There are three theatre spaces, a cinema, café, bar and art galleries and, alongside its own shows, it offers a rich and varied programme of visual arts, film, theatre, music, dance and comedy. Theatr Clwyd works extensively with the local community, schools and colleges and creates award-winning work for, with and by young people. In the past two years it has co-produced with the Sherman Theatre, Hijinx, Gagglebabble and The Other Room in Cardiff, Paines Plough, Vicky Graham Productions, HighTide, Hampstead Theatre, Bristol Old Vic, the Rose Theatre, Kingston, Headlong, Sheffield Theatres, the Orange Tree Theatre, English Touring Theatre and National Theatre, amongst others.

In 2016/17 over 420,000 people saw a Theatr Clwyd production, in the building and across the UK.

HOW TO SPOT AN ALIEN

A play for families

Georgia Christou

Characters

JELLY, *twelve years old*
JONJO, *eleven years old*
MUM
POLICEMAN
AUNT LEINA
RENNIE
P.A.-LIEN

Notes for Playing

For three or more actors.

– indicates an interruption.

… indicates a character not speaking the rest of their thought.

Jelly and Jonjo can speak to the audience whenever the text demands it.

References to TV shows, computer games, dances crazes, etc., can be updated as appropriate.

This text went to press before the end of rehearsals and so may differ slightly from the play as performed.

Lights up on JELLY *and her brother* JONJO.

1.

JELLY. Most kids' stories have a happy ending.

JONJO. This one, I'm afraid to tell you, does not.

JELLY. So if you like tales where good triumphs over evil

JONJO. And fluffy animals sing to princesses

JELLY. And no one dies a painful and gruesome death, then you best leave now.

JONJO. Here's your chance.

JELLY. Go on.

Beat.

Good.

JONJO. So now we've separated the cowards from the heroes

JELLY. And the raisins from the nuts

JONJO. We can begin.

JELLY. This story may not have a happy ending, but it does have a happy beginning.

JONJO. Picture a house

JELLY. Made of red bricks

JONJO. On a terraced street.

JELLY. The door is painted dark blue

JONJO. With a moon-shaped window.

JELLY. Inside are two kids.

Lights up on MUM.

MUM. Jelly?

JELLY. Yeah!

MUM. Jonjo?

JONJO. Coming. That woman you can see there is our –

JELLY. Mum?

MUM. Yes, love?

JELLY. If the Earth's spinning all the time why can't we feel it?

MUM. Because we're moving too.

JONJO. What are stars made of?

MUM. Gases mostly.

JELLY. You know the space in between the spiky bits of my
hairbrush?

MUM. Yeah.

JELLY. What's that called?

MUM. Just space I think. Now, bed, the pair of you.

She tucks them in.

JELLY. But –

MUM. Jelly, it's late…

JELLY. I've got a burning question. Like if I don't find out, I'm
literally gonna burst into flames. Is that what you want?

JONJO. Is it?

JELLY. Is it?

JONJO. Is it?

Beat.

MUM. Go on.

JELLY. What would happen if you fell into a black hole?

MUM. Really, before bed?

JONJO. Pleeeeease!

Beat.

MUM. No one really knows, because no one would live to tell the tale. But some people think you'd be... spaghettified.

JELLY. Spaghetti-what?

MUM. Oh yeah, laugh all you like. But it's a miserable way to go. Your body would be stretched like a rubber band.

JELLY. Then what?

MUM. Your arms would go one way, your feet going the other until you're...

JONJO. What?

MUM. Torn in half. And then in half again. And again and again until you're nothing... but a pile of spaghetti.

Beat.

JONJO. Cool.

JELLY. Wicked.

MUM. Now, sleep. Goodnight, you strange things.

JONJO. Love you to the moon and back.

JELLY. To the stars and beyond.

MUM. Love you the whole universe.

2.

JELLY. We wake up the next morning

JONJO. To a policeman standing at the end of our bed

JELLY. Which does not look like good news.

POLICEMAN. Children?

> *The* POLICEMAN *bends his knees.*

> I'm afraid to tell you that your mum

JELLY. Our mum

JONJO. Our brilliant

JELLY. Clever

JONJO. First-class mum

POLICEMAN. Has disappeared.

> *Beat.*

JELLY. Disappeared?

POLICEMAN. Yes, she left mysteriously in the night never to return again.

JELLY. Maybe she's gone to work?

JONJO. Or to get some milk?

JELLY. Or she's playing hide-and-seek? Did you think of that?

POLICEMAN. She left this –

JELLY. He pulls a note from his pocket.

POLICEMAN. *Dear children, I've disappeared mysteriously in the night never to return again. Signed, Mum.*

JELLY. This doesn't make sense.

JONJO. She couldn't –

JELLY. She wouldn't –

> *Beat.*

POLICEMAN. I'm afraid

JELLY. The policeman continues with a serious and solemn face

POLICEMAN. You're going to have to live at the orphanage.

JELLY. Now we've all seen enough kids' stories to know this is far from ideal.

JONJO. But we don't have anywhere else to go.

JELLY. As Mum has no family.

JONJO. So we pack our bags with our most precious possessions

JELLY. Which for Jonjo is his pet spider Albert, his Lady Gaga CD and his lucky rat's tail

JONJO. And for Jelly is her encyclopedia, a half-eaten Mars Bar she found under the bed –

JELLY. And Mum's pocket mirror.

JONJO. But Jelly's got one of her looks on her face. One of her looks which either means she's got wind or she's thinking.

JELLY. I've been thinking.

JONJO. Phew.

JELLY. Something about this doesn't smell right to me. We can't rely on anyone else. We're going to have to solve the mystery of Mum's disappearance ourselves.

JONJO. And then she screws up her face again and I know she's going to have another brilliant thought.

JONJO *screws up his face and holds his nose.*

Jelly!

JELLY. Sorry.

3.

JELLY. We sit on the doorstep with our bags –

JONJO. And wave goodbye to our house.

JELLY. For those of you that are getting all blubbery, we did warn you that this was not a happy story so cut it out.

JONJO. We turn to start the long walk to the orphanage –

AUNT LEINA *appears suddenly, as if out of nowhere.*

AUNT LEINA. There they are! My little puddings. Don't worry, Auntie's here now.

JELLY. Auntie?

AUNT LEINA. Why yes! I'm your Aunt Leina.

JONJO. Now this is the first we've heard of any Auntie, and so we tell her –

JELLY. This is the first we've heard of any Auntie.

AUNT LEINA. I am your mum's half-sister. Was, your mother's half-sister.

JELLY. Mum doesn't have a half-sister

JONJO. Says Jelly who's sharp as a pin with a needle on top.

AUNT LEINA. Of course you don't remember me. Why would you? When I've been away all this time, travelling round Europe and rescuing poor sick koala bears. Now let me look at you. My Jessie.

JONJO. Jelly.

AUNT LEINA. Not for me, thanks. And who's this, strapping young lad? It can't be. Is that my Django?

JELLY. Jonjo.

AUNT LEINA. Tell me, Django, where are you going with those enormous bags?

JONJO. The orphanage.

AUNT LEINA. Surely not?

JONJO. We have to.

JELLY. We don't have anywhere else to go.

AUNT LEINA. How awful for you both.

JELLY. We've had better mornings, yeah.

AUNT LEINA. Now I hope you don't think this is too… soon. But I was… wondering, well hoping really, that you might come to live at my house? With me.

Pause.

Forget it, it's a silly idea –

JONJO. We'll come!

JELLY. Jonjo!

JONJO. It's that or the orphanage.

JELLY. Have you lost the absolute plot?

JONJO. Have *you*?

JELLY. We've only just met her.

JONJO. So?

JELLY. So we don't know anything about her.

JONJO. We know she takes care of sick animals. And she seems… nice enough. Anyway, she's family, Jelly.

Beat.

AUNT LEINA. I'm going to get going, I should never have put you on the spot like that.

JELLY. We'd love to.

AUNT LEINA. You would?

JELLY. If the offer still stands?

AUNT LEINA. We're going to have so much fun!

JONJO. And so the decision is made.

AUNT LEINA. Children!

JELLY. We go to live with Aunt Leina.

4.

JELLY. The next thing we know we wake up in a bed

JONJO. In a room that we don't recognise.

JELLY. Jonjo, do you remember falling asleep?

JONJO. No. You?

JELLY. No. But then no one ever remembers falling asleep.

The sound of an electric drill.

What's that...?

JONJO. We find Aunt Leina

JELLY. Screwing bolts onto the front door.

AUNT LEINA. You're up! Did you sleep well?

She revs the drill in her hand.

Just a bit of extra security.

JELLY. Security?

AUNT LEINA. After all, we can't be too careful. If someone is out there disappearing people, then we can't take any chances.

JELLY. She tightens the last screw and hangs a bunch of keys around her neck.

Beat.

Aunt Leina?

AUNT LEINA. Yes, dear?

JELLY. What's up there?

JELLY *points up at a hatch in the ceiling.*

AUNT LEINA. The attic.

JONJO. Can we have a look?

AUNT LEINA. No!

JELLY. Why not?

AUNT LEINA. It's where I keep my collection of… poisonous snakes.

JONJO. Poisonous snakes?

AUNT LEINA. Yes, they have free rein so don't come crying to me if one of them bites you. Now –

JONJO. Aunt Leina?

AUNT LEINA. Yes… my love?

JONJO. Why are the windows painted black?

AUNT LEINA. To protect you.

JELLY. Protect us from what?

AUNT LEINA. I'd hate for you to go the same way as your mother.

JONJO. Aunt Leina?

AUNT LEINA. My my, you do ask a lot of –

JONJO. Who do you think would win in a fight between Spiderman and Bruce Lee?

AUNT LEINA. I don't –

JELLY. Aunt Leina?

AUNT LEINA. WHAT!?

Beat.

JELLY. Ah I've forgotten what I was going to ask now.

Beat.

Oh yeah I've remembered, if the world was going to be taken over by killer cockroaches, would you a) go underground, b) invest in some super-strength insect repellent or c) –

AUNT LEINA. What is that?

Beat.

There. Sticking out of your pocket?

JELLY. Oh. It's Mum's.

AUNT LEINA. You know I can't possibly let you keep it.

JELLY. But it's mine.

AUNT LEINA. Mirrors are quite dangerous for children of your size.

JONJO. Dangerous?

AUNT LEINA. Too much staring in the mirror will turn your eyes yellow. I thought everyone knew that? Now hand it over.

JELLY. No!

Beat.

Thanks. I just… I'd rather keep it with me.

AUNT LEINA. Perhaps now may be a good time to run through the rules?

AUNT LEINA *claps twice.*

JONJO. A bedsheet uncurls round the room like a roll of wrapping paper.

JELLY. Written on it in pink lipstick:

JONJO. 'HOUSE RULES.'

AUNT LEINA. Just a few to keep you safe. Jelly, if you would?

JELLY. 'Number one…'

Beat.

AUNT LEINA *nods encouragingly.*

'Always wash behind your ears. Unwashed ears will turn mouldy and drop off.'

AUNT LEINA. Happened to a child I knew. Unfortunate, to say the least.

JONJO. 'Number two: No bad behaviour. Bad behaviour rots your teeth.'

JELLY. 'Number three: No questions'?

JONJO. 'Every time a child asks a question a squirrel dies.'

JELLY. Is this a joke?

AUNT LEINA. That depends. Are dead squirrels funny?

JONJO. 'Four: Thinking may only take place outside the house.'

JELLY. 'Number five:'

JONJO. 'No leaving the house.'

JELLY. How are we supposed to stop thinking?

AUNT LEINA. It's for your own good. Thinking is the root cause of all fungal foot infections.

JELLY. But it's impossible.

AUNT LEINA. Jelly, I hope you're not challenging my authority?

Beat.

What does it say there plain as yogurt on the wall? 'Number nineteen.'

JELLY. 'No challenging Aunt Leina's authority.'

AUNT LEINA. Indeed. Now, the mirror if you would.

JELLY *hands over the mirror.*

Rules are rules I'm afraid.

Beat.

Don't look at me like that, *I* didn't make them up.

5.

JELLY. That afternoon we make a plan.

Jonjo. We have to find Mum. That policeman couldn't find a pig in a henhouse.

JONJO. Good point.

JELLY. We're gonna have to find her ourselves. We should start by making a list of all the places she might be.

AUNT LEINA. Knock knock.

AUNT LEINA *enters*.

What are you beavering away at in here? I was going to see if you'd like to join me for afternoon tea but I can see you're busy.

AUNT LEINA *turns to exit*.

JONJO. Afternoon tea?

JELLY. We'd love to we really would –

JONJO. We could… probably take a short break?

AUNT LEINA *produces a huge tower of cakes all piled up on a twenty-five-tiered cake stand.*

The KIDS *eat and eat and eat.*

Time passes.

AUNT LEINA. You're sure I can't get you another scone? Macaroon? Mini cheesecake?

JONJO. I'm stuffed.

AUNT LEINA. How about a bit of telly, to aid digestion?

JELLY. We'd better get to work. Mum's not gonna find herself, is she.

AUNT LEINA. You're quite right. I have always admired a good work ethic. Britain's Most Talented Canines can wait.

JONJO. Britain's Most Talented…

AUNT LEINA. Canines dear. It's a TV show. Silly really. There's a dog who can rap the whole alphabet. While dancing the tango.

JONJO. I've never seen a dog dance the tango.

AUNT LEINA. That's exactly what Amanda Holden said. But no, you carry on. I'll just have it on quiet in the background.

She switches the TV on.

The KIDS *get drawn towards the TV.*

The theme tune begins.

Time passes.

JELLY. We really do need to get back to –

AUNT LEINA. I can't, I won't, I refuse to believe it. Strictly Come Salsa Celebrity Special!

Time passes.

The channel changes.

I'm A Bit Famous On Ice.

Time passes.

The channel changes.

Super Cop Car Chase.

Time passes.

The channel changes.

Antiques Quiz of the Year!

The channel changes.

Time passes and passes and passes.

The TV glares on the KIDS' *faces.*

JELLY. Jonjo…

…was there something we were meant to…

…remember?

6.

JELLY. Now we're not proud of what you just saw.

JONJO. Not in the slightest. In fact we're ashamed to say things stayed like that for months.

JELLY. And we'd probably still be there now

JONJO. Watching Rodents Do the Funniest Things

JELLY. If it weren't for The Dream. I know there are few things as boring as listening to someone else's dreams, so I'll make it quick. I'm in Paris and there's a koala bear sitting on top of the Eiffel Tower.

MUM. Jelly? Jonjo?

JELLY. I look around but I can't see her. Mum?

MUM. Jelly?

JELLY. Mum, where are you?

MUM. Jelly, can you hear me?

JELLY. And her voice gets further and further away like she's under water or on a different… Jonjo! Jonjo!

JONJO (*half-asleep*). What?

JELLY. Koala bears do not live in Europe.

JONJO. Is that some kind of riddle?

JELLY. Hand me my encyclopedia.

He does.

Leina said that she'd been looking after sick koalas in Europe, but look, I knew it!

She shoves the book under his nose.

JONJO. Interesting… what do you think this means?

JELLY. It means… Aunt Leina tells lies.

7.

JONJO. Mum says you always have to tell the truth even if it's the hard thing to do.

JELLY. She says you have to be able to look in the mirror each morning and face yourself.

JONJO. We're not exactly sure what that means but it sounds like good advice.

JELLY. We find Aunt Leina in the kitchen.

AUNT LEINA. Good morning, my little cherubs!

JELLY (*to* JONJO). Remember. Like we practised.

> JONJO *gives* JELLY *a thumbs-up*.

AUNT LEINA. I spose you're after some brekkie pops?

JELLY. You hear that, Jonjo?

JONJO. I hear that, Jelly.

JELLY. She thinks we want 'brekkie pops'.

AUNT LEINA. Well do you?

JONJO. Oh Leina.

AUNT LEINA. What?

JONJO. Leina, Leina, Leina. Take a seat.

JELLY. Jonjo says, channelling all the bad cops he's ever watched on the telly.

AUNT LEINA. Why are you being all –

JELLY. I've been thinking.

JONJO. And Jelly sips a cup of coffee that is a) prepared especially for this moment and, b) –

JELLY. Disgusting.

AUNT LEINA. Thinking?

JELLY. Yeah, you know, me and Jonjo we were hanging around, chewing the fat.

JONJO. When a little birdie tells me that things round here might not be exactly as they seem. Capeesh?

AUNT LEINA. I'm sorry?

JELLY. My brother

JONJO. Colleague!

JELLY. My colleague and I have reason to believe that you haven't been entirely honest with us.

JONJO. We need something from you. To aid our investigation.

AUNT LEINA. And what exactly is that?

JONJO. The truth!

JELLY. And Jonjo slams his fist down on an imaginary desk.

JONJO. Why did you lie to us about tending to sick koalas?

AUNT LEINA. Now really, Jonjo –

JELLY. Don't act all innocent with me. You said on the day you arrived at our house, quote

JONJO. 'I have been travelling in Europe rescuing sick koala bears'

JELLY. Unquote.

JONJO. Can you explain to us why, when we investigated this further we found koalas ARE ONLY NATIVE TO

JELLY. AUSTRALIA.

JONJO. What are you hiding, Leina? What explanation could you possibly have?

AUNT LEINA. I was in a zoo.

JONJO. Pardon?

AUNT LEINA. I was working in a zoo.

JELLY. A zoo?

AUNT LEINA. Yes. Now. I have got a Victoria sponge in the oven and a pot of jam on the boil –

JELLY. Wait! What about Mum?

AUNT LEINA. What about her?

JELLY. The great unsolved mystery of her disappearance.

AUNT LEINA. That's not for you to worry about, dear.

JELLY. Well, someone has to. The police aren't doing anything.
And her own half-sister doesn't give a monkey's tail where
she is. In fact you can't even talk about Mum without
looking like a boiling kettle.

Beat.

AUNT LEINA. You're right.

JELLY. I am?

AUNT LEINA. I've done this all wrong. Stupid stupid woman
that I am.

JELLY. I'm glad to see we're finally sipping through the same
straw.

AUNT LEINA. You know, I've only ever wanted to keep you
safe and happy. But I suppose you're not babies, it's time
you knew the truth.

JELLY. That's all we want.

AUNT LEINA. I've kept it from you all this time, I didn't want
to hurt your feelings, you see…

JONJO. You won't.

JELLY. We promise.

AUNT LEINA. Fine. Your mother is…

JELLY. What?

JONJO. Where is she?

AUNT LEINA. Dead.

Beat.

JONJO. Dead?

AUNT LEINA. I wanted to tell you I really did –

JONJO. Dead?

AUNT LEINA. I found out a few months back. I just couldn't face telling you, I didn't know how –

JONJO. I'm going to my room.

JONJO *exits*.

AUNT LEINA. Jonjo love. Oh dear.

Pause.

I really am so sorry, Jelly.

JELLY. How did it, how did she…?

AUNT LEINA. An accident. Tragic accident, involving an escaped convict and a runaway train.

JELLY (*almost to herself*). Accident?

AUNT LEINA. Now I'm going to make us a nice hot –

JELLY. She left a note.

Beat.

AUNT LEINA. What?

JELLY. That day.

AUNT LEINA. I don't think we ought to keep running through the –

JELLY. The policeman read us a note. From Mum.

AUNT LEINA. So?

JELLY. So she would never have written a note if she was in an accident.

AUNT LEINA. Perhaps you should have a lie-down.

JELLY. What really happened to our mum?

Beat.

AUNT LEINA. I told you, she –

JELLY. I don't believe you.

AUNT LEINA. Go to your room now please.

JELLY. Is anything that comes out of your mouth even true?

A fizzling sound comes from AUNT LEINA.

AUNT LEINA. I've tried to keep this civil –

JELLY. I asked you a question.

Steam is starting to rise from AUNT LEINA's *body.*

AUNT LEINA. You've upset your brother.

JELLY. You're the one who upsets him. With your filthy –

AUNT LEINA. I'm warning you –

JELLY. Stinking –

AUNT LEINA. Angelica –

JELLY. Pack of –

AUNT LEINA. Enough –

JELLY. Lies!

A flash of light and a splitting sound like a new world being born.

For a moment AUNT LEINA *isn't there, the image of a ten-foot monster stands in her place.*

It roars an ear-splitting roar. Then scuttles away.

Now it's a strange experience realising your sole and chief guardian is some kind of terrifying monster. You'd think you'd shout 'Run for your life!' Or 'Take cover!' Or – 'Take that, monster sole and chief guardian.' But what actually happens is a) you wet yourself a bit. And b) you turn and walk slowly to your bedroom where you sit in shocked silence.

Pause.

JELLY *and* JONJO's *room.*

Jonjo. You won't believe what I just saw.

8.

JELLY. The thing is, it turns out he actually *won't* believe it.

JONJO. A monster?

JELLY. With claws and scales and –

JONJO. Jelly…

JELLY. I think I even saw a tentacle!

JONJO. Right.

JELLY. I swear, Jonjo.

JONJO. Why are you doing this?

JELLY. I'm not doing anything, I'm telling the truth.

JONJO. If you're trying to save my feelings –

JELLY. I don't give a monkey's knickers about your feelings.

> *Beat.*

> Which isn't true but he's being so annoying I want to squirt lemon in his eyes.

> JONJO *is crawling around the room.*

> What are you doing?

JONJO. I've lost Albert.

JELLY. How can you be thinking about your stupid spider at a time like this?

JONJO. He's not just a spider, he's a stunt spider, they're not easy to come by. Besides, I think maybe this is a good thing.

JELLY. Our aunt being some kind of monster is a good thing?

JONJO. Now we know that Mum's…

> *Beat.*

> Well, we can stop looking for her now, can't we.

> *A knock on the bedroom door.*

AUNT LEINA (*off*). Kids?

JELLY. Barricade the door!

JONJO. What are you –

JELLY. Don't let her in, Jonjo. Her teeth, her eyes, her claws –

AUNT LEINA *enters, looking perfectly normal.*

AUNT LEINA. There we go, my little treacle tarts.

JELLY. But…

AUNT LEINA. Warm milk and honey. It's good for a shock.

She exits.

JONJO. Doesn't look much like a monster to me?

JELLY. Maybe she changed back?

JONJO. Listen, Jelly. This is our life now. So, like her or not, we better get used to it.

9.

That night. JONJO *is on his hands and knees, looking under the bed.*

JONJO. Albert?

Beat.

Albert?

Jelly and Aunt Leina are both asleep and snoring like a pair of rhinos. Normally when I can't sleep I have a chat with Albert and we practise some stunts. But I've looked all over the house, in cupboards, under beds, I even braved Aunt Leina's underwear drawer. There's only one place I haven't looked.

He looks up.

I sneak into the attic, holding only my lucky rat's tail for protection from the poisonous snakes.

In the attic.

Albert. Albert?

A spider crawls across the floor.

Albert!

JONJO *chases after him.*

Come back, come on, mate. It's me!

He crawls under a pile of magazines, and then under a big dust sheet which is covering… something?

JONJO *pulls the sheet off to reveal a shiny silver spaceship.*

He reaches out and touches the ship. It hums with life.

He retracts his hand. He moves away. The spaceship moves towards him.

He moves towards the ship, the ship moves back. Like a dance or a conversation.

What are you?

AUNT LEINA (*off*). Jonjo?

He scoops up his spider off the floor.

JONJO. Coming!

10.

JONJO. Jelly, I need to talk to you.

JELLY. I'm busy.

JONJO. Doing what?

JELLY. Watching Rise and Shine Britain.

JONJO. You hate that programme.

JELLY. Well, this is my new life and I'm accepting it. Now shhhh, I'm trying to learn how not to look like a lumpy sausage in a dress.

JONJO. You don't even own a dress.

I can tell she's still in a mood with me for two reasons. Number one, she keeps saying she's fine –

JELLY. I'm fine.

JONJO. And number two she has a face like a slapped chicken. Listen, last night I broke into the attic –

JELLY. Have you lost the absolute plot?

JONJO. No I –

JELLY. What about the snakes? Wait let me guess. No / snakes

JONJO. Snakes, exactly.

JELLY. That lying, cheating –

JONJO. But I *did* find something else in there. Something that looked like a s–

AUNT LEINA *enters*.

AUNT LEINA. Jonjo. Why aren't you eating your custard?

JONJO. I am, Aunt Leina.

JELLY. It's lovely, Aunt Leina.

JONJO. Extra… crunchy.

AUNT LEINA. And how are you finding the programme? Absorbing? Entertaining?

JELLY. Boring.

AUNT LEINA. Hmmm.

AUNT LEINA *scribbles in a notebook and exits.*

JONJO. Where were we?

JELLY. Oh yeah. The attic.

JONJO. I'm about a hundred and ten per cent sure what I found in the attic last night is… a spaceship.

Beat.

Now if I'm right, which I'm sure I am, that means Aunt Leina isn't just your regular everyday kind of monster. It means, she's an –

JELLY. Alien?

Beat.

JONJO. What you thinking?

JELLY. I mean, it's ridiculous, it's crazy it's…

JONJO. Completely and absolutely spot on?

JELLY. Yeah.

Beat.

And I spose it explains the whole…

JELLY *makes the sound of* AUNT LEINA *turning into an alien.*

JONJO. Sorry I didn't believe you.

JELLY. No problem. Sorry I put toenail clippings in your custard.

JONJO. What?

JELLY. Never mind. Jonjo, what do we know about Leina?

JONJO. Apart from the fact she's a big fat alien liar-pants.

JELLY. Apart from that.

JONJO. She makes good snacks?

JELLY. She takes kids, kids who don't have parents. Right?

JONJO. Right.

JELLY. But why?

JONJO. Maybe she's lonely... maybe there's no other aliens on Earth and she wants some company.

JELLY. I don't think so. I think she wants something with us. The question is, what?

JONJO. I don't wanna stick around to find out. So we decide to do what any self-respecting kid would do in this situation.

JELLY. We decide to run away.

JELLY. Aunt Leina keeps the keys to the front door on a chain around her neck.

JONJO. We need to get those keys.

JELLY. Tonight!

Night falls.

The KIDS *look at each other and nod.*

They creep into AUNT LEINA*'s room where she's flat-out. The* KIDS *creep closer.*

AUNT LEINA *lets out a big snore.*

They freeze. Then creep closer still.

AUNT LEINA *rolls over.*

JELLY *takes the keys from around her neck.*

They do a small victory dance.

She snores again.

Finally we reach the door, dodge the laser

JONJO. Padlock

JELLY. Bolts

JONJO. Two locks

JELLY. One more to go.

JONJO. Wait.

JELLY. What is it?

JONJO. Albert! I've lost –

JELLY. Got him.

> JELLY *hands* JONJO *his spider.*

> Couldn't go leaving a stunt-spider behind, could we? Come on.

> AUNT LEINA *appears as if out of nowhere.*

AUNT LEINA. Where do you think you're going?

JONJO. Let me handle this. Listen, Leina. We've had a great time, you've been very hospitable for the most part but we're starting to feel like this set-up might not be for us. So thanks for everything, good luck and you know –

JELLY. Au revoir, you flipping freakshow.

JONJO. Just couldn't resist, could you.

AUNT LEINA. Now you know I can't let you out there, don't you?

JELLY. Why, cos it's so 'dangerous'?

JONJO. Cos you're 'protecting' us?

JELLY. Sing another tune. I saw you, remember. I know what you are. So you can keep pretending like you're Mary flipping Poppins but we know the truth.

AUNT LEINA. And what's that?

JELLY. That if Pinocchio and ET had an evil love child, it would equal you. Come on, Jonjo.

> *The sound of the bolts closing on the door behind them.*

> You can't keep us locked in here forever.

AUNT LEINA. You're right. You're becoming far too good at escaping. I'll have to find somewhere else to put you. Somewhere extra-secure. Now, into the cupboard.

JONJO. You what?

AUNT LEINA. You heard me.

JELLY. We won't.

AUNT LEINA. No?

JELLY. We don't have to do what you say.

AUNT LEINA. Are you sure about that? Walk.

JELLY *and* JONJO *start moving beyond their control.*

Spit spot!

They stop outside the kitchen cupboard.

In!

JONJO. What?

AUNT LEINA. What? Who? Why? How? Enjoy it while it lasts, kids. Oh yes I've got plans for you.

JONJO. What kind of plans?

AUNT LEINA. That...

JELLY. She says with an evil smile

AUNT LEINA. ...would be telling.

The KIDS *are shoved into the cupboard.*

The slam of the door.

11.

Inside the kitchen cupboard.

JONJO. I can't take this any more. The nights and the days are blurring into one. I can feel my stomach starting to eat itself, my muscles wasting away.

JELLY. At this point we've been in the cupboard half an hour.

JONJO. What's that?

JELLY. Mum's mirror. I grabbed it when we got the keys.

JONJO. Where d'you think she is now?

JELLY. I dunno. This is all we got of her right?

JONJO. Right.

JELLY. So maybe it'll tell us where she is?

JONJO. It's a mirror not a sat nav.

JELLY. Have you got any better ideas?

　　Beat.

　　That's what I thought. After three then. One, two…

　　They open the mirror.

　　JELLY *stares at her reflection.*

　　Who is that?

JONJO. Very funny.

　　Beat.

　　Are you running out of air or something? It's you.

　　JELLY *snaps the mirror shut.*

　　Give it here.

　　JONJO *looks in the mirror, then snaps it shut himself.*

JELLY. Jonjo, I don't think I've seen my reflection in weeks. Months maybe.

JONJO. I think through all the rooms in Aunt Leina's house. No bathroom mirror.

JELLY. No shiny spoons.

JONJO. No silver kettle.

JELLY. No shiny spoons.

Beat.

You have to be able to look yourself in the eye. It's what –

JONJO. Mum said, I know.

JELLY. So why can't we then?

JONJO. I didn't like what I saw.

JELLY. And what was that?

JONJO. –

JELLY. Fine I'll tell you what I saw. Two kids who've been pretending all along. If we really wanted to get out we'd have found a way ages ago. Because if we ever *do* get out we'll have to face the facts – that we've got no idea where Mum is or where to start looking or if she's even still alive?

JONJO. Stop it.

JELLY. Maybe we wanted to stay here cos it's nice and it's easy and there's a constant supply of TV and snacks.

Beat.

She's fattening us up. It's the only explanation. The only reason she'd have kept us this long.

JONJO. Oh god. You're right.

JELLY. I always am. Except when I'm wrong.

JONJO. I was sucked in.

JELLY. Jonjo?

JONJO. It's just so hard to resist.

JELLY. Jonjo…

JONJO. The sugary high. The comforting lull of the TV set.
  I've been a fool –

JELLY. Jonjo!

JONJO. What? I'm repenting here.

12.

JELLY. She's left the front door open.

JONJO. Don't lie to me, Jelly.

JELLY. I'm not – look.

  He puts his eye to the keyhole.

  You know what Mum used to say to us?

JONJO. Always change your pants on Tuesday?

JELLY. When you're in a tight spot, use what you've got. Jonjo,
  hand me that Lady Gaga CD.

  JELLY *picks the lock carefully. Then a satisfying 'click
  sound'. The cupboard door flies open and they tumble down
  onto the floor.*

  Go, Jonjo.

AUNT LEINA. Will you ever give up?

JELLY. Don't look like it!

JONJO. And we slam the door behind us.

AUNT LEINA. I warned you, you can't say I didn't warn you.

JONJO. And with that, we step out into the cool, dark night.

13.

JELLY. Freedom! I can taste it, Jonjo, and it tastes a thousand times better than junk food!

JONJO. For the first time in months I feel... light?

JONJO's feet are lifting off the ground.

JELLY. Now we just got to find Mum and... Jonjo? Oi... come back here.

JELLY's feet lift off the ground too.

I think we're...

JONJO. Floating!

JELLY. Floating away from that wretched, stinking old house.

JONJO. Floating away from Aunt Leina!

JELLY. Floating into... space. Wait.

JONJO. Weeheeeee!

JELLY. How do we stop?

JONJO. Why would you stop? It's like trampolining and holidays and nicking a sip of Mum's beer all at once.

JELLY. Aren't you listening? We're in space, you doughnut. And we're headed straight for a –

JONJO. Black hole!

The KIDS are dragged towards it.

JELLY. We have to get down.

JONJO. I'm trying.

JELLY. Come on.

JONJO. I can't stop it.

JELLY. Do you want to be spaghettified or what?

JONJO. I can't... breathe... Jelly –

JELLY. Grab hold of me.

JONJO. Jelly!

JELLY. Jonjo!

> *Everything goes black. A sound like a car horn.*

14.

A vehicle, like a VW camper-van-rocket hybrid comes screeching up next to the KIDS.

The horn beeps again.

RENNIE. Get in!

> *The* KIDS *get in the back of the van, spluttering, gasping.*

Shut the door, you're letting all the air out.

> JONJO *slams the door shut. They breathe deeply.*

JONJO. Jelly?

> JELLY *is slumped on the seat next to* JONJO.

What's wrong with her?

RENNIE. Low on oxygen.

JELLY. As my eyes start to focus I can see we're inside a vehicle, it reminds me of the old caravan our neighbour Rudi used to have parked on our street. Only I don't think his one could fly.

RENNIE. Deep breaths now, titcher. There we go.

JONJO. You're alright!

JELLY (*whisper*). Jonjo, we have to get out of this thing.

JONJO. We can't.

JELLY. I can feel the driver's eyes watching us. All eight of them.

RENNIE. Everything alright back there?

JELLY. / Fine.

JONJO. Fine.

JELLY. We've been abducted, tricked and fattened up for the slaughter by an alien who was treating us like a walking snack.

JONJO. What's your point?

JELLY. My point is, if one of them is like that...

Beat.

Let us out, child thief.

RENNIE. I'm sorry?

JELLY. We've just escaped one evil alien we're not about to run off into the sunset with another.

RENNIE. I'm not a child thief.

JONJO. I spose you like kids for your lunch, do you, child thief?

JELLY. Kiddy cruncher.

RENNIE. I'm not, I'm vegan I swear. Check my rubbish.

JONJO pulls out a carton from a rubbish bag.

JONJO. Oat milk.

Beat.

I think we're safe.

RENNIE. Of course you are. I rescued you, didn't I?

JELLY. Yeah well we've not had the best experience with aliens so far.

RENNIE. You know a rotten egg has the same shell as a good one.

JELLY. Thought you were vegan?

RENNIE. Ha! No getting past you is there. Now, we need to get away from Mendax, sharpish. If I get caught helping out human children... I dread to think what they'd do to us all.

JELLY. Mendax?

RENNIE. See the planet down there, the one glowing purple…

JELLY. No offence but we learnt all our planets in like Year 4.
    Jonjo?

JONJO. Mercuryvenusearthmars/jupiter

RENNIE. Get down.

JELLY. Saturnuranus/neptune

RENNIE. Under there, quick!

   Beat.

   Still as statues, titchers.

   The KIDS *duck as a searchlight passes over the van and
   shines into the windows.*

   JELLY *and* JONJO *don't even dare to breathe.*

   The light goes.

   Okay, the coast is clear. But we need to move fast. The place
   is swarming with security.

   The KIDS *emerge from the heap of rubbish.*

JELLY. Mendax?

RENNIE. It was my home.

JONJO. Where d'you live now?

RENNIE. Sleep in the van most nights. But it's better than that
    place. Since the CKK took over – the Curiosity Killed the
    Kids Party – slippery, slimy, terrible bunch. Lucky you got
    out when out did. If the rumours are true…

JELLY. What kind of rumours?

RENNIE. It's probably just talk. But I've heard they've got an
    invention. Something that's been made to… oh, titchers.

JONJO. We can handle it.

RENNIE (*sad*). That's been made to drain all the questions out of kids' minds. They're having their big meeting tonight. We should get you home.

JONJO. You can get us back to Earth?

RENNIE. Least I can do.

JELLY. Do you know where it is, this meeting?

RENNIE. Course. The Grand Hall.

JELLY. We have to get there –

RENNIE. Absolutely not. It's too dangerous.

JELLY. But –

JONJO. Jelly, we've spent months, maybe years up here. I'm starting to grow a beard it's been so long.

He rubs his chin.

JELLY. It's not a beard it's leftover porridge. We have to go back.

JONJO. Have you got a death wish?

JELLY. If we don't stop them we'll be as good as dead anyway.

JONJO. We'll tell people, we'll tell the Prime Minister, the Queen, the President –

JELLY. It'll be too late. Whatever they're doing, they're doing tonight. We have to stop them.

Beat.

RENNIE. I think you're forgetting who's in the driver's seat here. And it's a no from me.

JELLY. Listen, you couldn't stand it down there right?

RENNIE. No but –

JELLY. A world without questions.

JONJO. And while all the baked goods and entertainment is nice for a bit...

JELLY. You couldn't live like that.

Beat.

And we can't either.

Pause.

RENNIE. You know this is a crazy idea don't you?

JELLY *and* JONJO. Yep.

RENNIE. Let's get on with it then.

JELLY. You know this rubbish… can we borrow it?

RENNIE. Be my guest.

JONJO. And we zoom back towards the planet full of flesh-eating aliens. The very one we just escaped from.

15.

The screech of brakes.

RENNIE. The Grand Hall.

JONJO. We've stopped outside an enormous glass building.

JELLY. And by this time a plan is already forming in my head.

JONJO. Jelly has made us a disguise out of tin cans, old banana skins and some soya yogurt pots.

JELLY. It's not my best work but I am optimistic.

RENNIE. Are you sure about this?

JELLY. Sure as eggs are eggs and spiders have eight legs.
    Speaking of which –

JONJO. Albert?

JELLY. He must be here somewhere.

JONJO *shakes his head.*

I'm so sorry, Jonjo.

JONJO. Rest in space, my friend. Rest in space.

Beat.

RENNIE. I'll have all my fingers and eyes crossed for you. Good luck.

The camper-van flies away into the night sky.

JELLY. We better get inside. Now just act normal. And when I say normal I mean like

JONJO. A complete and absolute freaky nightmare.

JELLY. Exactly.

JONJO. We join the crowd, hundreds of aliens are piling into the place.

JELLY. Big ones –

JONJO. Small ones –

JELLY. Some with seven heads.

JONJO. We follow them into a round auditorium.

JONJO. Jelly, the windows.

JELLY. What about them?

JONJO. They're blacked out – just like Aunt Leina's. Look.

JELLY. He's right. In fact, every wall of this great glass building is covered in heavy curtains. They probably don't want anyone knowing what they're doing in here.

P.A.-LIEN. Settle down, please, settle down! It's my pleasure to welcome to the stage, Head of Innovation and Child Extermination of the Curiosity Killed The Kids party, Professor Fakesnew.

JONJO. The crowd erupts into applause

JELLY. Cheering

JONJO. Whistling.

JELLY. A creature walks up onto stage

JONJO. Tapping a claw along with her entrance music.

JELLY. It can't be.

JONJO. It is.

JELLY *and* JONJO. Aunt Leina!

AUNT LEINA *taps the microphone*.

AUNT LEINA. It is a well-known truth that there is no bigger threat to our species than human children. The itsy witsy little snot buckets are noticing everything, utilising search engines and staring up at the sky with wonder. These curious children grow into curious adults, astronauts, scientists, pioneers, threatening our home and our very existence!

JONJO. Hear, hear.

JELLY. What are you doing?

JONJO. Getting into character.

AUNT LEINA. Of course we have a long history of identifying the most curious children on Earth and tearing them from the planet. But sometimes a child get overlooked. For example, can anyone explain to me how it came to be that celebrity star-gazer Brian Cox was allowed to mature into adulthood on Earth?

JELLY. Her eyes scan the room.

JONJO. Elaine. Please stand.

JONJO. An enormous slug

JELLY. Wearing pearl earrings

JONJO. Stands with a squelch.

AUNT LEINA. Elaine, you were our representative for the north-west.

JONJO. Elaine's silver-grey body is shaking.

AUNT LEINA. Well? How did you miss him?

JELLY. Elaine hangs her slimy head in shame.

AUNT LEINA. We can't afford mistakes.

JONJO. She clicks her claws and two aliens carry a bucket of salt and throw it over Elaine.

JELLY. Who sizzles

JONJO. And bubbles

JELLY. And screams in pain.

JONJO. Before the guards carry her scorched remains out.

AUNT LEINA. I hope this has sent a clear message about how incompetence will be dealt with from here on in. Today, two Earth children escaped from my house.

JELLY. The crowd gasps

JONJO. Someone in the front row faints and has to be stretchered out.

AUNT LEINA. Of course they'll be long gone, swallowed by our great vast universe. I've kept them in my home for Earth-months and Earth-months. Studying their behaviour. Experimenting on them. And from my research I have created this –

JONJO. She pulls a DVD out of her pocket.

AUNT LEINA. On here is a programme I have created for public broadcast all around the world. The addict-ability of Love Island, the bingeosity of Breaking Bad and a theme tune so catchy that it will wiggle into your head like a worm and get stuck there forever! No Earth child will ever be able to look away from their television sets again!

JELLY. We have to stop her.

JONJO. How?

AUNT LEINA. Of course, the brains of curious children are tough and chewy. The more idiotic the child the better the brain is. For consumption.

JELLY. Consumption?

AUNT LEINA. And once we've frazzled their thinkers, they'll be easy pickings. Like gulls plucking stupid fish out the sea. We can feast!

ALIEN ONE (*voice-over*). I like mine chopped and fried in a pan.

ALIEN TWO (*voice-over*). I like mine steamed.

JONJO. I like mine deep-fried

JELLY. Shouts Jonjo, doing a brilliant job of blending in.

Beat.

AUNT LEINA. Deep-fried?

JONJO. Oh yeah. Dead good that.

AUNT LEINA. What's your name?

JONJO. Erm… Shrek.

JELLY. He wasn't an alien, you idiot.

JONJO. Course he was.

JELLY. He was an ogre.

AUNT LEINA. Stand up, Shrek. Let me see you.

The KIDS *stand, still in their disguise.*

It was my understanding that children cannot be deep-fried without affecting the delicate balance of flavours.

JONJO. No you're right, but if you errr…

JONJO *starts itching and wriggling in the costume.*

JELLY (*whisper*). What are you doing?

JONJO (*whisper*). There's something… [in my costume]

If you blanche it first.

JELLY. Stop wriggling, you idiot.

JONJO. Then sauté.

JELLY. Jonjo, keep still.

JONJO (*whisper*). I'm trying.

Then erm, add ketchup –

JELLY. But Jonjo can't stop wriggling and itching and squirming, a tin can clatters to the floor

JONJO. The yogurt pots ping off

JELLY. And our disguise is nothing more than a single banana skin laying on my head.

JONJO. Albert Einstein!

JONJO *cradles him close.*

Beat.

What now?

AUNT LEINA. Now now, dear. What have I told you about questions? Seize them!

The KIDS *are tied up on stage.*

In an unexpected turn of events, the subjects of my experiment are now available again. You'll be able to see with your own eyes the results of my brilliant programme.

Beat.

Bring out the TV!

JELLY. The guards wheel in a TV the size of a horse.

A mind-numbing theme tune rings around the hall.

Jonjo, close your eyes.

JONJO. I can't.

JELLY. Think about something else. Anything. Think about nine-times-eighteen. Think about osmosis. Think about... Jonjo?

AUNT LEINA. Don't you get it? By time I'm done with you, you won't even know your own names. You wouldn't recognise your own reflection.

JELLY. That's it! Hey, Leina!

JELLY pulls the pocket mirror out and holds it up to AUNT LEINA*, who, catching sight of herself screams in pain.*

Jonjo. The TV!

JONJO. Got it. Lucky rat's tail.

The rat's tail becomes a lasso and he uses it to pull over the TV with a crash.

AUNT LEINA. Give me that mirror!

The mirror floats up high into the air. It hovers above them before smashing to the ground.

JELLY. No!

AUNT LEINA. Nice try, Angelica. If you'd have just sat and watched the television like good little children you wouldn't have felt a thing, but, as you wish… now you'll be wide awake when I slice you open.

JELLY. So here we are.

JONJO. The end of our story.

JELLY. For those of you with weak stomachs…

JONJO. You were warned.

JELLY. I squeeze my eyes tight shut and wait for a sharp claw to dig into my skull, only there's something niggling, one word I can't get out my head…

WHY?

Beat.

AUNT LEINA. What did you say?

JELLY. You heard.

AUNT LEINA. You know this is exactly the kind of behaviour that landed you here in the first place.

JELLY. I don't care. If I'm gonna get munched alive I want to know why.

AUNT LEINA. Because... (*Turns and addresses the conference.*) children are cruel, heartless, dangerous beasts from which we must protect ourselves.

JELLY. Right only the thing is, we're not.

AUNT LEINA. Quiet, you.

JELLY. Me and Jonjo, we're nothing like that.

JONJO. You know we're not.

JELLY. The fact of the matter is –

AUNT LEINA. Facts. You think anyone cares about the boring old facts? Aliens are the same as people. They want a story. A hero – that's me. And an evil villain to be saved from – that's the pair of you.

JONJO. We're not evil.

AUNT LEINA. You are if I say you are.

AUNT LEINA *lets out a cry of pain for the benefit of her audience.*

You see, everybody, what these cruel children have done to me? She's burning me with her laser eyes.

JONJO. Are you?

JELLY. I don't have laser eyes, you doughnut! She's tricking them –

Another cry of pain from AUNT LEINA.

AUNT LEINA. He's torturing me with his dark magic!

JONJO *looks down at his hands confused.*

JELLY. ...Just like she tricked us. She hates kids for the same reason she hates questions and the same reason she can't stand to look in the mirror.

Beat.

They all show up the truth.

AUNT LEINA. Hurry, we must stop them before they can do any more damage. Help yourself everyone. Feast!

JONJO. And this is it.

JELLY. The aliens rise from their seats

JONJO. Lick their lips

JELLY. And close in around us.

JELLY. Jonjo. You know what to do?

JONJO. Sure as eggs is eggs.

The KIDS *run at the* ALIENS, *who scatter in fear.*

JELLY. We pull back the curtains.

Light fills the space.

AUNT LEINA. No!

AUNT LEINA *catches sight of herself in the glass walls.*

No!

She turns away but she can see her reflection everywhere. Her skin sizzles, her head crackles. She cries out in pain.

JELLY. And so it came to pass

JONJO. That our not-Aunt Leina and a hundred flesh-eating aliens

JELLY. Finally faced themselves, reflected in the glass walls of the great Grand Hall.

JONJO. Just before she disappeared into the atmosphere she looked at us and said one word

AUNT LEINA. Why?

JONJO. And then she was gone.

Pause.

We did it, Jelly!

16.

JONJO. We defeated Leina.

JELLY. I know.

JONJO. We saved the world from the flesh-eaters.

JELLY. I know. It's brilliant, Jonjo.

JONJO. So why don't you look happy?

JELLY. I am, of course I am. It's just... we're no closer to finding Mum.

JONJO. Course we are.

JELLY. What do you mean?

JONJO. I think maybe your brain's a bit fried.

Beat.

Mum didn't go anywhere, dumbo. We did.

JELLY. You mean, you think we should look... [at home]

JONJO. It's as good a place to start as any.

JELLY. One small problem. How we gonna get there?

JONJO whistles.

The KIDS *look out the windows.*

Nothing.

JONJO (*disappointed*). It was worth a try.

JELLY. Jonjo, look.

The spaceship from AUNT LEINA*'s attic lands in The Grand Hall.*

JONJO. You came? Hello, mate!

The ship hums with life and they step inside.

The whole stage becomes the inside of a spaceship.

JELLY. Now I don't know if you've ever launched a spaceship but if you haven't I can tell you now, it's pretty flipping brilliant.

The spaceship takes off.

The universe passes them by outside the window, they wave at a camper-van in the distance.

We're nearly at the end of the story.

JONJO. Which might not have such an unhappy ending after all. Eh, Albert?

JELLY. Jonjo?

JONJO. Jelly?

JELLY. I can't get something out my head.

JONJO. Is it 'Poker Face' cos I feel exactly the same.

JELLY. No. Okay yeah but… what if there's more of them out there? Or on Earth even. They could be anyone. Doing any job, anywhere in the universe.

JONJO. They're not all bad, remember.

JELLY. So how do you tell?

JONJO. Easy. Keep your wits about you. And a shiny spoon in your sock for emergencies.

Beat.

Look!

He points out of the window.

See far below us

JELLY. But getting closer by the second…

JONJO. Is a red-brick house

JELLY. With a blue door

JONJO. And a moon-shaped window.

JELLY. Inside is a woman

JONJO. Who's been there all along.

JELLY. She's been calling her kids' names for so long she never expected them to answer.

MUM steps out into the garden and looks up at the sky.

MUM. Jonjo? Jelly?

The KIDS appear behind her.

JELLY. Mum?

She turns, just as the lights –

Blackout.

End.

A Nick Hern Book

How To Spot An Alien first published in Great Britain as a paperback original in 2018 by Nick Hern Books Limited, The Glasshouse, 49a Goldhawk Road, London W12 8QP, in association with Paines Plough and Theatr Clwyd

How To Spot An Alien copyright © 2018 Georgia Christou

Georgia Christou has asserted her right to be identified as the author of this work

Cover: illustration: Sam Ailey; design: Thread Design

Designed and typeset by Nick Hern Books, London
Printed in the UK by Mimeo Ltd, Huntingdon, Cambridgeshire PE29 6XX

A CIP catalogue record for this book is available from the British Library

ISBN 978 1 84842 786 0

www.nickhernbooks.co.uk

facebook.com/nickhernbooks

twitter.com/nickhernbooks